LANGUAGE ARTS EXPLORER

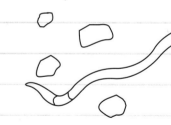

SOIL

by David M. Barker

SCIENCE LAB:
SOIL

CHERRY LAKE PUBLISHING • ANN ARBOR, MICHIGAN

CHERRY LAKE Publishing

Published in the United States of America
by Cherry Lake Publishing
Ann Arbor, Michigan
www.cherrylakepublishing.com

Printed in the United States of America
Corporate Graphics Inc
September 2011
CLFA09

Consultants: Lynn Dudley, professor and chair, Department of Earth, Ocean, and Atmospheric Science, Florida State University; Gail Saunders-Smith, associate professor of literacy, Beeghly College of Education, Youngstown State University

Editorial direction:
Lisa Owings

Book design and illustration:
Craig Hinton

Photo credits: Fotolia, cover, 1, 5; Stephen Ausmus/USDA, 7, 10, 12; USDA, 8, 27; Peggy Greb/USDA, 16; Red Line Editorial, 17, 20, 22, 24; Vitaliy Pakhnyushchyy/Big Stock, 18

Copyright ©2012 by Cherry Lake Publishing
All rights reserved. No part of this book may be reproduced or utilized in any form or by any means without written permission from the publisher.

Library of Congress Cataloging-in-Publication Data
Barker, David, 1959-
Science lab. Soil / by David M. Barker.
    p. cm. – (Language arts explorer. Science lab)
ISBN 978-1-61080-207-9 – ISBN 978-1-61080-296-3 (pbk.)
1. Soils–Juvenile literature. I. Title. II. Title: Soil.
S591.3.B37 2011
631.4–dc22

                        2011015133

Cherry Lake Publishing would like to acknowledge the work of The Partnership for 21st Century Skills. Please visit www.21stCenturySkills.org for more information.

TABLE OF CONTENTS

You are being given a mission. The facts in What You Know will help you accomplish it. Remember the clues from What You Know while you are reading the story. The clues and the story will help you answer the questions at the end of the book. Have fun on this adventure!

Your mission is to dig up the secrets of soil. You walk on soil, or dirt, every day. Why is soil important? Are there different kinds of soil? Can soil help fight climate change? How do scientists measure differences between soils, and what kinds of experiments do they do? How do plants affect soil? Read the facts in What You Know, and start your mission to uncover the world of soil.

WHAT YOU KNOW

★ **Soil** is sand, silt, and clay mixed with decaying plants and animals. Some scientists include living organisms such as **bacteria** and **fungi** in their definition of soil.

★ Humans depend on soil to grow their food.

★ Some soils contain enough nutrients to grow plants. Other soils contain few nutrients.

Soils are important for supporting life, growing food, keeping the environment stable, and much more.

Calvin Collins is learning the ropes in a soil science laboratory and in the field. Carry out your mission by following his journal entries.

I am working with Dr. Jane Robinson and her soil science team. We are heading out to three locations today to learn about soil. I ask Dr. Robinson what we will be doing when we get there. "We are trying to answer some basic questions about the soils in this area," she replies.

"Isn't it all just the same dirt under there?" I ask.

"I think you'll be surprised what we find when we look," she responds. "It's a whole other world down below." Underground soil cities flash through my mind. Dr. Robinson asks, "What do you think is under there? Make a prediction, and we'll see if you're correct." I predict there will be dirt, stones, roots, and worms.

"We should see all those things," she says, "but I think we'll find other interesting things too. Today we'll be looking under a farm field, a prairie, and a forest."

Farm Field

When we arrive at the field, we talk to Mr. Hall, the farmer who owns it. He tells us he used to grow corn in this field. The team chooses three places in the field to dig. The holes will be about three feet by four feet (1 m by 1.2 m) and four feet (1.2 m) deep with straight walls. While some

Farmers like Mr. Hall can control the amounts of moisture, nutrients, and living things in their soil.

members of the team dig, others hand out equipment. My job is to take plastic bags and a box of tins to each hole. The tins will hold soil samples to take back to the lab.

When the holes are dug, Dr. Robinson shows me what we've uncovered. She is kneeling in a hole and invites me to have a closer look. "As you can see, you were right. Dirt, roots, stones, and probably even some worms are down here." I imagine my underground cities full of worms and bugs. "Do you notice anything interesting about the soil as you look from the top to the bottom of the hole?" asks Dr. Robinson. I notice different colors in the soil, and I see they form a pattern. "The layers?" I ask.

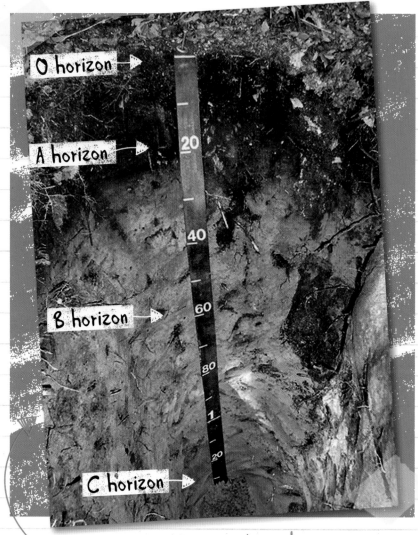

O horizon →

A horizon →

20

40

B horizon →

60

80

1

20

C horizon →

Most soils have the same basic layers, or horizons. The O horizon is on top, followed by the A, B, and C horizons.

Soil Horizons

"Exactly," replies Dr. Robinson. She explains that all soils have layers, called horizons. Most soils have the same basic horizons. Soils form over hundreds of years, becoming deeper over time. Plants, animals, and chemical reactions change the soil as it forms. Plants add nutrients and decaying material from the top. Rainwater seeps down through the soil. The water carries some substances down with it and leaves others behind. Eventually, these changes make the horizons. The horizons make up the **soil profile**.

Dr. Robinson points to the top inch (2.5 cm) of our farm soil profile and says, "This is the O horizon. What do you think it's made of?" I tell her it looks like a bunch of roots and rotting plants. "That's right," she says. "The O horizon is not really soil. It is mostly plant material. Bacteria and fungi in the soil break this material into smaller pieces. *O stands for organic*, which means 'from something living.'"

She points to the next layer, the A horizon. It is dark, sticky looking, and about ten inches (25 cm) deep. Dr. Robinson says this is where most of the roots are and where worms, ants, beetles, and other animals live. There is a lot of oxygen in this layer. It is also full of decaying plant material.

Beneath the A horizon is a lighter-colored reddish layer. It is the B horizon. Dr. Robinson explains, "This layer does not have much organic material. The reddish color is from rust washed down by water. Under the B horizon is the C horizon, which is near the bottom of the hole and looks

Each type of soil has a different profile. Soil profiles can teach us about a soil's properties and how the soil formed.

like sand, gravel, and stones." Dr. Robinson describes this as the rock the soil first formed on.

The team takes soil samples from each hole at different depths. They put the samples in the tins I brought them and seal the tins into labeled plastic bags. They also take photographs of the soil profile with a tape measure in the picture to show depths. Finally, all the holes are refilled, and the sod is placed on top like before.

Prairie

I travel with Dr. Robinson to the next site. While we are driving, she explains where we are going. "This site is a prairie. Prairies are grasslands where climate, fires, and grazing animals keep trees from growing. Prairies once covered much of North America, but now they are almost

HOW SOILS FORM

Five things affect the way soils form:

1. The parent material is the material from which a soil forms. It is usually carried from somewhere else by water or wind. It can also form from broken-down rock.

2. Rain, wind, and changes in temperature break down parent material and change how fast soil forms. Rainwater washes materials through the layers of soil.

3. Plants add material to the soil they grow in. Animals and microorganisms break down this material.

4. The slope of the land affects the amount of sun and moisture soils get and whether they are easily washed away.

5. Soils take time to change.

Prairie fires kill trees and clear out dead plants.
The ash provides nutrients for prairie grasses.

gone. Because prairies have such fertile soil, most have
been cleared for farmland. There are still a few large areas
of prairie left in the middle of the continent. Today we are
visiting a prairie that has been growing for 30 years. The
prairie managers burn it regularly, which is part of what
keeps a prairie healthy."

The prairie looks like the farm field to me, except the
plants are taller. I ask Dr. Robinson whether the soil profile
will look the same as the one in the farm field. "Let's test
that hypothesis by digging," she replies.

We dig holes, gather samples, and photograph the soil profile as we did in the farm field. The prairie profile has similar horizons to the profile we saw at the farm. The dark A horizon is thicker here though. Dr. Robinson says this is because grass roots grow deeper and denser than crop roots.

Forest

Next we move to the forest site. Dr. Robinson explains, "This forest was cut down a hundred years ago and has been growing back ever since. Most of the trees are deciduous. That means they lose their leaves in winter."

Again, we get to work digging holes. The forest soil profile is much different than the farm field and prairie. This time, the A horizon is thin. I predicted it would be thicker here because of all those tree roots, but I was wrong. When I ask Dr. Robinson to explain, she says that forest plants have much more material above ground than below, so less organic material gets into the soil. Prairie plants have dense root systems, so most of their material is underground. ★

A week later, I am visiting the soil science team again. Dr. Robinson says we are going to measure the **soil texture** of the samples we collected last week, starting with the samples from Mr. Hall's field. I begin to take notes.

Sand, Silt, and Clay

Dr. Robinson explains that soil texture is the amount of sand, silt, and clay in a soil. The amounts of these ingredients affect how the soil feels when you touch it. Silt particles are much smaller than grains of sand, and clay particles are even tinier. Clay is what gives soil its stickiness.

A soil's texture affects what can grow and live in it. Soils with a lot of clay hold nutrients that help plants grow. They also hold water well. This means clay soils are great for growing plants in dry climates, but they may not be good for plants in moist climates. Soils with a lot of sand allow water to drain quickly, which is good for plants in wet areas. But sandy soils can dry out easily. The larger sand grains leave plenty of space for air, which all plants need to grow. Soils with a lot of silt and clay are in danger of being washed away.

MAKING SAND, SILT, AND CLAY

Rocks are broken into smaller particles in a process called weathering. Weathering can be chemical, physical, or biological. Chemical weathering happens when chemicals in water and air help to break rock down. Physical weathering happens when objects carried by water or wind scrape against the rock. Biological weathering happens when plants grow on rocks and break them down with the force of their growing roots. All of these processes can produce sand, silt, and clay.

Measuring Soil Texture

This is how Dr. Robinson's technician, Claire, measured soil texture: First, she sifted the soil through a screen. The screen let sand and anything smaller through. Then she took this fine soil and dried it in an oven. Claire put the dried soil in a container with water. She shook the container, and after waiting exactly ten seconds, Claire removed a small amount of the cloudy liquid on top. She said that ten seconds allowed the sand to settle out, so this mixture contained only water, silt, and clay. She dried this sample and weighed the silt and clay.

Then she stirred the mixture again, and we let it sit for eight hours. At the end of the day, Claire took another sample of the cloudy water from the top. She said enough

You can discover a soil's texture by weighing its dry ingredients.

time had passed for the silt to settle out of the water, so this sample contained only clay. I knew what the next step would be. She just had to dry and weigh the clay-only sample and subtract it from the silt-plus-clay weight to know how much silt there was. The last step was to weigh the sand left in the container.

We discovered that our farm soil had 50 percent silt, 35 percent clay, and 15 percent sand. I plotted these numbers on the chart soil scientists use to describe soil texture. Our soil was a silty clay **loam**. Loams are soils that contain medium amounts of sand, silt, and clay. Loams are the best soils for growing crops. ★

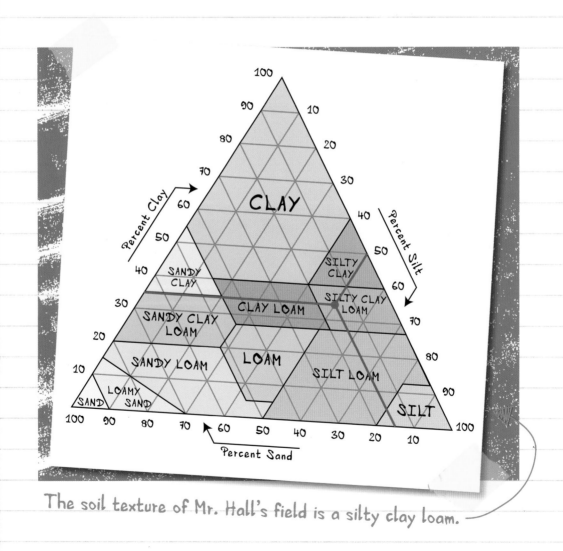

The soil texture of Mr. Hall's field is a silty clay loam.

This week, we will be learning about soil microorganisms in the lab. Dr. Robinson tells me that bacteria and fungi are examples of microorganisms. They are living things that are too small to see without a microscope. Plants do not grow well in soil without microorganisms. Bacteria and fungi break down dead plants and turn them into food for other plants. Soil bacteria are especially important. They capture gases from the atmosphere and turn them into nutrients that plant roots can absorb.

Earthworms help bacteria and fungi break down dead plants, and you don't need a microscope to see them.

CROP ROTATION

Farmers plant different crops in different years so the crops grow better. Crop rotation decreases pests, including harmful soil organisms, by taking away the plants they like every year. It also keeps the soil's nutrients in balance. Crop rotations usually include a year when legumes such as peas and beans are grown. Legumes have places in their roots where bacteria can grow. These bacteria take nitrogen gas out of the air and change it into a form plants can use. Nitrogen is a vital nutrient for all plants. Growing a legume adds nitrogen to the soil for the next year's plants.

Rick is the technician studying these microorganisms. "Today we will be testing the prairie and forest soils to learn about the bacteria and fungi in each type of soil," he says.

"Are we going to count the bacteria?" I ask. This seems like a long, slow job, so I am hoping Rick has something else in mind.

"There are ways of counting them," he says, "but we're going to use another method. We are going to see how much they are breathing." I ask if that will tell us how many bacteria there are. Rick says not exactly, but we will be able to compare how many microorganisms are in the soil samples from each site.

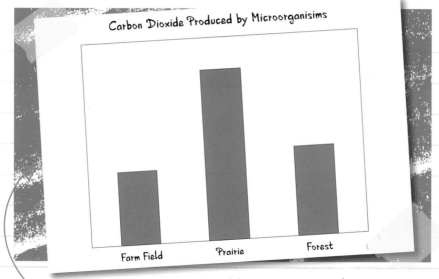

Carbon dioxide produced by microorganisms in farm field, prairie, and forest soils

Measuring Microorganism Activity

This is how Rick tested the soil: First, he put the soil through a screen to take out all the large pieces. Then he divided the soil into two samples. To one sample, he added a chemical that killed all the bacteria and fungi. This sample was for comparison. Rick called it the **control**. Then he mixed both samples with water and added sugar to them. The sugar is food for the microorganisms. He sealed the samples in tubes and placed them in a warm, dark place for six hours.

Rick used a machine to measure the amount of carbon dioxide the microorganisms breathed out. We calculated how active they had been, or roughly how many there were. I made a bar chart to show the results. The prairie soil had much more microorganism activity than the other soils! ★

Dr. Robinson asks me what I know about carbon. I tell her it is an element, that our bodies contain a lot of carbon, and that there is something called a carbon cycle. She agrees with all of these points. *Not bad*, I think.

Carbon and Climate Change

"The carbon dioxide gas in the atmosphere is part of the carbon cycle," Dr. Robinson says. "Scientists are interested in carbon dioxide because it affects climate change. We think climate change, or global warming, is happening because humans are burning fuel and cutting down forests. These actions put carbon dioxide into the air. Carbon dioxide traps extra heat in the atmosphere, which can harm the whole planet."

"What does this have to do with soil?" I ask.

"Good question," she replies. "Soil holds a lot of carbon. The carbon in the soil will eventually end up in the atmosphere as carbon dioxide. This is an important part of the carbon cycle. By learning about the carbon in the soils around here, we can understand the role of our soils in climate change and the carbon cycle."

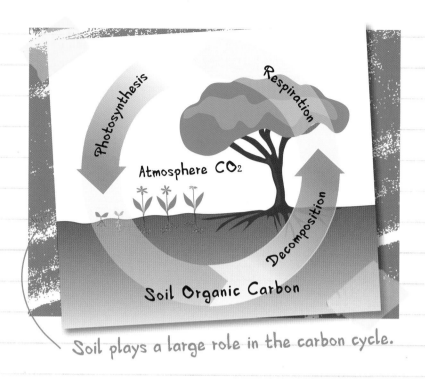

Soil plays a large role in the carbon cycle.

The Carbon Cycle

Claire walks into the room, and Dr. Robinson asks her to explain what she knows about the carbon cycle. Claire smiles and says, "Plants take carbon dioxide from the atmosphere and use it to make food. Then animals eat plants, using the carbon from those plants in their own bodies. When the plants or animals die, their bodies decay, releasing the carbon into the atmosphere as carbon dioxide. Fuels such as coal and oil also hold a lot of carbon. We are releasing the carbon in coal and oil quickly, which is why people are worried about climate change."

Dr. Robinson adds, "These are the most important parts of the carbon cycle for us. When plants die and decay, their **organic carbon** enters the soil. The carbon stays there for a while before it goes back into the atmosphere. That is the piece of the puzzle we are looking at. By finding out how much organic carbon is in each soil type, we can understand how farm field, prairie, and forest soils might affect Earth's climate. Which type of soil do you think holds the most carbon?"

I think for a moment and say, "I predict that the forest soil will have the most carbon."

Dr. Robinson says, "You are starting to think like a scientist. That is an interesting hypothesis. Why will the forest soil have the most?"

"There is more plant material above ground, so there will be more organic carbon underground."

CARBON IN FARM SOILS

Scientists estimate that farm soils in the United States store 22 million tons (20 million tonnes) of carbon. They believe that with changes in farming methods, this number could climb to more than 220 million tons (200 million tonnes). Farmers can help increase soil carbon by not plowing their fields. Without plowing, the soil does not mix with the air as much, so more of the soil's carbon stays in the ground.

Dr. Robinson says, "We will be able to test that hypothesis when we compare the soils in the lab."

This is getting exciting, I think to myself.

Measuring Soil Carbon

Dr. Robinson did the organic carbon measurements herself this time. She began by sifting the soil samples in the same way as the others. Then she mixed the soil with a chemical that sticks to organic carbon and boiled the mixture. After about two hours, she slowly added another

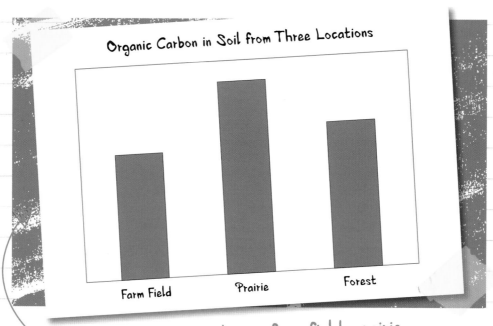

Amounts of organic carbon in farm field, prairie, and forest soils

chemical until the color of the mixture changed to bright green. The amount she had to add before it turned green told us how much organic carbon was in the soil sample.

Dr. Robinson then showed me the results from the different soil samples so we could compare them. I made a graph to show the differences.

"What do these results tell us?" I ask Dr. Robinson.

"Our results and the results from other studies show that prairie soils store a lot of carbon," she replies. "But this is just a small part of the story. Scientists estimate that soils hold more than twice as much carbon as the atmosphere. We believe we can use soils to reduce the rate of climate change. For example, if we work to restore prairies, more carbon dioxide will be trapped in prairie soil and unable to escape into the atmosphere."

"I guess my prediction was wrong," I say.

"All that matters is that you asked the question in the first place," she replies. "Science is not about being right. It's about learning, and to learn we have to ask questions and find the answers. Answers that don't match our predictions sometimes tell us more than answers that do." ★

Congratulations! You have completed your investigation of the underground world of soils. You discovered that soils have different layers called horizons, which make up their soil profiles. Soils can also have different textures, or amounts of sand, silt, and clay. A soil's texture affects the plants that grow in it. You found that different soils have different amounts of microorganisms. Microorganisms provide plants with nutrients by breaking down organic material. You also discovered that soils play an important role in the carbon cycle.

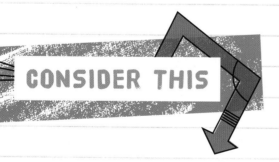

CONSIDER THIS

★ What are the five things that make each soil the way it is?

★ Describe the layers in a soil profile. How are the layers in farm field, prairie, and forest soils different?

★ Which soil type had the most organic carbon in it?

- ★ Which of the soils discussed in this book would be best at fighting global warming and why?
- ★ What soil texture would be good for a plant that needs a lot of water to grow? What soil texture would be good for a plant that doesn't grow well in wet soil?

The best way to learn about soil is to get your hands dirty. What discoveries can you dig up?

bacteria (bak-TEER-ee-uh) single-celled organisms that can be seen only with a microscope

carbon dioxide (kahr-buhn dye-AHK-side) a gas formed from carbon and oxygen; carbon dioxide gas traps heat in Earth's atmosphere

control (kuhn-TROHL) the part of an experiment used for comparison

fungi (FUHN-jye) a group of organisms that feed on other organisms; molds and mushrooms are fungi

horizon (huh-RYE-zuhn) a layer in a soil profile

loam (LOHM) a soil with nearly equal amounts of sand, silt, and clay

microorganism (mye-kroh-OR-guh-niz-uhm) an organism that cannot be seen clearly without a microscope

organic carbon (or-ga-nik KAHR-buhn) carbon compounds that come from living things

soil (SOIL) a mixture of sand, silt, clay, and decaying plant and animal matter

soil profile (SOIL proh-file) a vertical section of soil from the ground's surface to the rock the soil formed on

soil texture (SOIL teks-chur) the amounts of sand, silt, and clay in a soil

LEARN MORE

BOOKS

Faulkner, Rebecca. *Soil*. Chicago: Raintree, 2007.

Franchino, Vicky. *Super Cool Science Experiments: Soil*.
Ann Arbor, MI: Cherry Lake, 2010.

Lindbo, David L., et al. *Soil! Get the Inside Scoop*. Madison,
WI: Soil Science Society of America, 2008.

Taylor-Butler, Christine. *Experiments With Soil*. Chicago:
Heinemann Library, 2012.

WEB SITES

Dr. Dirt's K-12 Teaching Resources

http://www.wtamu.edu/~crobinson/DrDirt.htm

Do activities based on scientific methods to study soil.

Soil Science Education Home Page

http://soil.gsfc.nasa.gov

Visit this site from NASA to learn more about soils.

Soil Science Society of America

https://www.soils.org/lessons

Check out resources for students interested in
studying soils.

FURTHER MISSIONS

WORM WATCH

Find a glass container and use a piece of cardboard to divide it in half. You'll have earthworms living on one side and plain soil on the other. Pour sand or gravel into the bottom of the container. Put soil with little organic material in the middle and some ground-up dead leaves on top. Add worms to one side, and keep the habitats moist. Watch what happens for at least a week, and record your observations. How do worms change the soil's layers? What happens to the soil texture? How does the color of the soil change? Did anything change on the side without worms?

NEW HORIZONS

Investigate your own soil. Find a place to dig into the soil at your school or at home. Make sure you get permission first. The hole does not need to be very deep to find the change from the A horizon to the B horizon. Write a description or take photographs of the soil horizons. Does the soil profile look like any of the ones discussed in this book? What is the soil's texture like? Does it have more sand, silt, or clay? Would plants grow well in this soil? Why or why not?

INDEX

ABOUT THE AUTHOR

David Barker obtained his doctorate in zoology at the University of Texas at Austin. Since then, Dr. Barker has taught and worked as an editor and writer of educational products in print and on the Web. He lives in Texas.

ABOUT THE CONSULTANTS

Dr. Lynn Dudley earned a PhD in soil science from Washington State University in 1983. Since then he has been teaching college students about soils and continuing his research. In 2006, he joined the faculty of Florida State University as a professor of geological sciences and is now the chair of the Department of Earth, Ocean, and Atmospheric Science.

Gail Saunders-Smith is a former classroom teacher and Reading Recovery teacher leader. Currently she teaches literacy courses at Youngstown State University in Ohio. Gail is the author of many books for children and three professional books for teachers.